THE BOY OF MANY MIRACLES

(And My Spiritual Journey as a Result)

Beverly Anne Munyon

ISBN 979-8-88644-608-1 (Paperback)
ISBN 979-8-88644-609-8 (Digital)

Covenant Books
11661 Hwy 707
Murrells Inlet, SC 29576
www.covenantbooks.com

I'd like to dedicate this book

First to The Glory of God and His Faithfulness

To the Baratta family who unselfishly gave Samuel a chance to live

And to our dear friend, Fr John Dreher, for his love, prayers, guidance and support on this journey

My daughter was married on June 5, 1999. It was a beautiful day, and she was marrying a wonderful young man. Everything was perfect.

Two months later, she conceived her first child. She learned that it was a boy. He would be our first grandson. We had two older granddaughters. As you can imagine, we prayed for a good pregnancy and a healthy baby. It never once dawned on us that the baby might be anything but perfectly healthy.

Samuel was born on April 24, 2000, at 10:24 p.m. during an emergency C-section. Tom and I had watched helplessly as Marie labored for twenty-four hours trying to give birth to her son. After the C-section, Tom came out holding Samuel (8 lbs., 2 oz.) and put him in my arms. My husband and I marveled at this perfectly healthy little boy and thanked God for this gift of life. Exhilarated and exhausted, we returned home and tried to sleep.

Tom called around 1:00 a.m. to say that Samuel was on a little oxygen. Just a precautionary measure, we were told. He was having just a bit of trouble breathing. We went in at 6:00 a.m. to see him again. He did not look too well, and they had transferred him to intensive care. All sorts of tubes and machines were around him. I tried to go to work but couldn't. I returned to the hospital. Things only got worse. We were told not to touch him because they had him asleep and did not want us to stimulate him. My God, what had happened to our perfectly healthy baby? What was wrong? No one knew.

Now meetings with doctors took place and then talk of a gas trial that he was going to go on. One minute it looked like things were getting better; the next minute, it appeared he wouldn't live. Two days after his birth, on April 26, we were advised to get him baptized. Fr. Giudice came to the intensive care unit, and Dave and I and Tom and Marie stood around this swollen baby who was in an induced sleep and watched as Father baptized him. We were all numb. This wasn't how it was supposed to happen. Marie and I had bought and written out his baptismal invitations before Samuel was born. What was happening? We focused on being with Samuel and caring for and supporting our daughter and son-in-law. The doctors began to be in touch with doctors at Massachusetts General Hospital. They were now deciding the fate for Samuel. Things went from bad to worse. Saturday came, and it was now time for Marie to be discharged from the hospital. She didn't want to leave without Samuel. It was decided that Tom and Marie would stay at our home to be closer to the hospital. Sunday came; it was Mercy Sunday. In Rome, St. Faustina was being canonized. Dave and I went to the cathedral after visiting with Samuel. I sought out Fr. Giudice and told him how badly things were going. He told me to let Samuel go; perhaps it wasn't meant for him to live. I cried and cried and told him, "*No, he must live!*" I found out months later that at every confession that Father heard that day, he gave praying for Samuel as a penance. During the Mass, he told everyone about Samuel and asked for their prayers.

All this time and the following week, I had no peace. I was exhausted, afraid, numb. I had much difficulty praying. I suspected but did not want to admit that I was disappointed with God. All this could have been avoided. Samuel could have been born perfectly healthy, but God, in His infinite wisdom, permitted Samuel to be born with many physical problems. I finally got on my knees in my prayer room before the crucifix and told God how disappointed I was but that I would try to trust Him. Then my peace returned to me.

No one seemed to know what Samuel's problems were, except that he probably wouldn't live. Then there was talk of Samuel being transferred to Massachusetts General Hospital in Boston to be hooked up to an ECMO machine to try to save his life. (ECMO = a heart and lung bypass machine. All of Samuel's blood was taken out, and oxygen was put back into it. And that kept getting repeated.) I begged God through prayer, fasting, and many tears to heal him without the trip to Boston. Early Friday morning (Samuel was almost ten days old), Fr. John called. He had just gotten back from Rome after attending the canonization of St. Faustina. He had just learned about Samuel, and we arranged to meet at the hospital that afternoon so he could anoint Samuel. For some reason, my soul was flooded with peace that morning, and I kept telling God that I would try my best to trust Him no matter what the outcome.

When Fr. John and I arrived at the hospital on that beautiful sunny day of May, Dr. Reddy met us as we entered the intensive care unit. He told me that Samuel had to leave for Boston in one hour. They could wait no longer. He was in critical condition, and an ECMO machine had just become available at Massachusetts General Hospital. I was in shock. Father prayed over Samuel's swollen body. He was yellow by now. Father gave us a prayer card from St. Faustina's canonization that we clung to throughout this ordeal. We begged God for His mercy. This time I didn't tell God how to show us His mercy. I just asked Him to cover us in His mercy in whatever form He chose.

Within a very short time, we whisked ourselves home and threw some clothes in a bag. Some toiletries were added, a few phone calls, and off we went to meet the ambulance at the hospital. As we locked the door, not one of us had a clue how long it would be before we returned. We arrived to see a doctor, nurse, and Samuel (all wired up) entering the ambulance. Tom and Marie followed in their car, and we followed behind. When we arrived at Massachusetts General Hospital, Samuel was already in the intensive care unit, being examined by the doctors. We met Tom and Marie in the waiting room. The doctor came with papers for Tom and Marie to sign and explained that they would examine him and see if he needed to be on an ECMO machine. As the doctor was speaking, another doctor burst into the room and said that they had to operate immediately because they were losing Samuel. They were going to operate and do a V-V. It was dangerous in Samuel's condition, and they told Tom and Marie to go and say goodbye to him. We waited for hours. No one was saying a word, but all of us were praying. Finally, we were told that he had made it through the operation, and the next twenty-four to forty-eight hours were critical. They were kind enough to let us stay in a small room that we could fit two chairs in. Tom and Marie slept sitting in a chair, and I lay on the floor. There wasn't enough room for Dave, so he went into the parking garage and tried to sleep in the van. In the middle of the night, there came a dreadful knock at the door. It was one of the nurses. Samuel had taken a turn for the worse, and the only way to try to save him was to do another dangerous operation, a V-A. It was extremely dangerous but had to be done immediately. While Tom and Marie were trying to take all this in, another nurse came and told them to hurry if they wanted to say goodbye. Tom and Marie were again allowed in for one minute to see their little boy. By now, he was almost unrecognizable; that is how bad he was. We paged Dave 911, and the four of us began a twelve-hour prayer vigil. After twelve hours, someone came out and said that he was still alive but very, very critical.

When we were finally allowed to see Samuel, he was almost unrecognizable. He was attached to so many machines and wires that unless you saw it for yourself, it would be hard to imagine. A full-time nurse and full-time respiratory therapist were assigned to watch him closely twenty-four hours a day. This time, much to our delight, we were encouraged to touch him, stroke his head, and hold his little fingers. We each took turns doing this amid the tangle of wires and tubes. Some days the fluid had gone to the top of his head, and it was shaped like a cone. At other times, it was to one side of his face, and it was very disfigured. At other times, his whole face was so swollen;

you could barely see his eyes. All this time, his skin was becoming more and more yellow (actually orange). So this is what the next three weeks of our life consisted of: taking turns holding his little finger and speaking softly to him, stroking his head, and telling him he was doing great and how much we loved him. When we weren't doing that, we sat in a tiny waiting room and prayed. This was our life! The average time for a child to be on an ECMO machine is five to seven days. Each day after that is extremely dangerous. All sorts of things can happen that will cause the child to die. The doctors tried many times to take Samuel off the ECMO machine after the seventh day, but each time met with failure. His little body could not make it on its own. A dialysis machine was now brought in to help pull some of the fluid off him. His lungs collapsed. They put a chest tube in. They collapsed again. A second chest tube was put in, then again and again. Four chest tubes were now inserted. We were told that if they collapsed gain, that would be the end. No more chest tubes could be inserted. There would be nothing more they could do. All this time, we were learning to trust God on a deeper level. One by one, we each surrendered ourselves and our little boy to God. We trusted Him to have mercy on all of us. Another answered prayer: His lungs did not collapse again at this time.

Before I continue, it might be helpful if I tell of an incident that happened two days after Samuel was brought to Boston and put on the ECMO machine. It was Sunday. We had arrived in Boston on the previous Friday. The four of us hadn't had much sleep in the past two weeks. The last few days had been especially difficult. We found a beautiful church just around the corner from the hospital. It was called St. Joseph's Church. We all went to Mass that Sunday morning. Little did we know that this church was to become a spiritual haven for us during the next four months.

The doctors had urged us to go for a walk to get some air. Samuel was very critical but stable. They would page us if we were needed. We reluctantly agreed, and off we went. We kind of wandered around, not knowing the area. We were very tired, hungry, and heavyhearted. I can even remember that we walked with our heads down. Suddenly, we heard shouts of joy and people clapping. We all looked up and saw people on either side of us, cheering us on, congratulating us, and clapping. They were all smiling. As we took a few more steps, someone came to each of us, congratulated us, and gave us each an ice cream. We had no idea what was going on. As we stepped to the side of this crowd to eat our ice cream (which we devoured. We were so hungry), we saw what was really happening. There had been some sort of race, and we had inadvertently walked across the finish line. The crowd naturally thought we had finished the race and were congratulating us. As we realized this, we all had a good laugh, the first in a long time! However, some days later, our loving God brought this scene back to me but this time on a spiritual level. He had "allowed" this event to happen very early on in our bedside prayer vigil of Samuel. He showed me that this was what was waiting at the end of this ordeal. No matter what happened, whether Samuel lived or died, the saints and the angels (the whole crowd of heavenly hosts) were there cheering us on. And as we crossed the finish line of this time of testing, they would be there to congratulate us for trusting God and staying close to Him as we learned to surrender all to His loving mercy. We *would* make it! With God's help, we would get through the cross and experience the resurrection!

I must mention, at this time, how good the hospital staff was to all of us. They were kind enough to supply a very small room for us to stay in. It had no windows, but it did have two chairs for Tom and Marie to sleep on so they could be next to Samuel. The hospital only had a limited number of rooms, and they were available to the parents of the children only. However, seeing our need, they gave Dave and I two cots and told us, if we could fit them in this tiny room, we would be allowed to stay there with Tom and Marie so we could all be together for support.

I forgot to mention something that happened a few days after Samuel's birth that was very significant. A friend of my mom's (Sr. Roberta) gave us some holy oil from St. Joseph's Oratory in Montreal, Canada. Br. Andre Bessette used to encourage the sick to pray for healing and to rub this oil on the affected area. Many, many people were healed. We started rubbing this oil on Samuel. We prayed for the intercession of St. Joseph and the Blessed Mother. During our hospital stay, we were given two books. We each read both of them. One of them was the story of Blessed Andre Bessette's life and work at St Joseph's Oratory. The other book was about St. Padre Pio. It was encouraging for us to read about the sufferings and trials they went through in their lives. Both these books were used by God to encourage us and give us much hope. We promised St. Joseph that if Samuel lived, we would all make a pilgrimage with Samuel to St. Joseph's Oratory in Canada to thank him for his intercession. (We did this along with Samuel's brother, Stephen, on the Feast of the Sacred Heart in June of 2002.)

The next several weeks were spent in much of the same manner. Dave and I got up early, went to see Samuel, and then attended morning Mass at St. Joseph's Church. We would then pick up a coffee and spend the morning in prayer in the waiting room. During this time, we were back and forth holding Samuel's fingers and speaking to him. We used to tell him all kinds of things. We told him everything that was going on—if we were going for a walk, what the weather was, that he was doing a great job, and he had to get strong and well because Dave and he were going fishing together, and there were so many things Grandpa wanted to teach Samuel. Of course, Samuel was still in an induced coma because of the ECMO machine. After nineteen days of ECMO, he was finally able to come off this machine. He had made it through against all the odds. However, now came a whole new set of problems. Because he had been on ECMO for such a long period, the doctor was no longer able to reconnect his carotid artery. He had to tie it. Now that Samuel was off the ECMO machine, his swollen body gradually returned to normal. The end result was a very tiny, beautiful, but very orange one-month-old baby. Shortly after his one-month birthday, Samuel's team of doctors/nurses took all tubes off him long enough for my daughter to hold her son for the very first time. It was a couple of days before her twenty-seventh birthday, and oh, what a birthday present to cradle her son in her arms for the first time since he had been born. Within minutes, however, he was taken away to have many tubes put back into his tiny body.

Over the next couple of weeks, test after test after test were performed on Samuel to find the root cause of all his many problems. They repeated many of the tests over and over again to be sure they were getting accurate results. During this time, the intensity and frequency of our prayers kept increasing.

Samuel had a feeding tube in him, and Marie wanted to try to breastfeed him. Time after time, she tried, but he did not have the strength to suck. They tried all sorts of methods with very little success. Much to Marie's dismay, Samuel had to remain on the feeding tube every three hours for four months. During this time, Marie brought in all sorts of outfits and baby clothes that she had bought for Samuel before he was born. She started each day by dressing Samuel in a different outfit. Tom and Marie were taking an extremely active part in their son's day-to-day needs. It became routine that, one by one, each of the nurses and doctors would find their way over to Samuel's crib to see how he was dressed. This was great for Marie's spirits. Tom and Marie took over much of the care for their son at this time. Marie was present each time the doctors came near her son. She listened and then asked questions. The nurse in her had all sorts of questions. When Samuel went down for tests, Tom or Marie always went with him. He never went alone. For our part, Dave and I stayed with Samuel when his parents needed a break. When we weren't with Samuel, we were usually praying.

While all this was going on inside the hospital, God was doing something else inside each of us. We were beginning to fear less and trust more. We were becoming stronger during this ordeal as we realized that we truly could draw our strength each day from our Father in heaven. He lovingly was caring for all our needs. We were beginning to understand that our loving Father loved Samuel much more than any of us could ever love him. I, personally, began to experience myself being wrapped in the arms of God, my Father. No one could touch me there; I was safe in His arms. It was at this time that the Lord began a marvelous work in my poor soul.

The priests at St. Joseph's Church in Boston will never know how their sermons sustained and encouraged us in our time of suffering.

One day, at daily Mass, an older priest said something I will never forget. It had a profound influence on me. He said that, one day, he was asked by someone if he was happy. He answered back immediately that, yes, indeed he was very happy. Then he was asked what made him happy. Why was he happy? He thought long and hard about that question. He finally smiled and came up with his answer. He was happy for one reason only: His happiness came from the fact that he belonged to God, and God belonged to him. That was it! It made me start asking myself the question: Was I happy? How could I be? My grandson was fighting for his life, my own life was on hold (or so I thought), and I had to stand by and watch my daughter and son-in-law suffer incredibly. This surely was not a time to be happy. But over the next few days, that question continued to nag me: Are you happy, Beverly? My answer continued to be, "How can I be happy at this time in my life?" As I continued to pray and do a lot of soul-searching, I heard God speak to me. He told me that he wanted me to be happy now and every day of my life. If I would allow Him, He would teach me how to be happy in the midst of any type of circumstance, and He would also teach me to dance. I did not understand this, nor how all this could be, but through grace, I gave my consent. I asked the Lord to come and teach me. I prayed to the Holy Spirit to give me a teachable spirit to enable me to truly learn these lessons well.

I vividly remember, one day, crossing the street, thinking how happy I would be if I was back to my "normal" life and if my life weren't on hold any longer. Immediately I heard God telling me that my life wasn't on hold. This is exactly where I was supposed to be at this particular time of my life. It was in this place at this time that He wanted me to be happy.

Another day, walking back to the hospital after morning Mass, I distinctly heard Jesus tell me that He wanted to teach me to dance.

Dance? Yes, He desired to teach me how to dance now, in Boston, while it appeared that my grandson was dying.

Well, that is exactly what began to happen. Each day after morning Mass, the Lord gave me dancing lessons. I began to learn that there is a dance for every kind of situation. Once I learned the steps, I could dance to any kind of music, whether joyful or sad. Through the different types of dances that Jesus taught me, I always looked down at His feet so I could follow. However, the last dance He taught me was different. It was a dance of trust. For this dance, I was forbidden to look down. I could only look up into Jesus's face and trust Him that he would glide me along. I never forgot this dance—the dance of trust is to always look into Jesus's face in the midst of terrible pain. My heart truly began to dance. I not only had a deep peace, I had indescribable joy, a type of joy that I had never known possible. My joy did not come from my circumstances (which were getting worse by the minute). Where did my joy come from? I could now honestly say with that elderly priest, "My joy, my happiness, comes from the fact that I belong to God, and He belongs to me." Nothing else truly mattered. Whether Samuel lived or died, whether I was home living a "normal" life or living in a six-by-twelve room in a hospital, my joy still came from that one fact: I belonged to my beloved, and my beloved belonged to me. It seemed so contradictory. At first I felt guilty. How could I have this much joy in the midst of so much sorrow? But God showed me that the two can indeed go hand in hand. In fact, it is His will that the two go hand in hand. Our circumstances will continue to change all throughout our lives, but the joy of the Lord is our strength and is never meant to change. This act of God brought me into much freedom. Even as I sat by the bedside of my grandson and watched his suffering, my heart had such a strange mix of sadness and sweet joy. God was indeed teaching me, and He was the best of teachers, ever so patient.

One day, one of the resident doctors told us that they had the results of all the tests, and they had diagnosed Samuel's illness. He casually mentioned that he had too much iron in his liver. Well we were kind of happy that they had finally figured out what was wrong.

I remember standing in front of the nurses' station with my daughter, and I was telling her that they would probably give us a prescription for medicine of some sort, and we would probably be taking him home in a couple of weeks. We were very happy the rest of that day.

The following day, we were notified that some of the doctors wanted to have a meeting with the four of us. We didn't know what to expect. We walked into a rather large room and saw four or five doctors, a couple of Samuel's nurses, and a social worker. We sat down, and one of the doctors began to speak. Dr. Vacanti told us that all the results were in from the many tests they did. They had good news and bad news. The good news was that they now knew what was wrong with Samuel. He was diagnosed with neonatal hemochromatosis (too much iron in the liver). The bad news was that they couldn't do anything for him. We were in shock! What did this mean? How could they not do anything for him? He went on to explain that the only way to fix this was to give Samuel a new liver. Yes, Samuel needed a liver transplant in order to live. We could barely take in what he was saying to us. The real bad news was that Samuel was not a candidate for a liver transplant. When my daughter recovered a bit, she asked why he wasn't a candidate. The doctor explained that Samuel had too many strikes against him. He was too little; he wasn't even two months old yet. Three of his vital organs had been affected: his liver, his kidneys, and his lungs. His lungs had collapsed over half a dozen times, and even now, he could not breathe on his own. His heart was working overtime to compensate for everything. His liver was completely destroyed. In fact, they told us that it was a miracle that Samuel was still alive. His liver was so destroyed and not functioning that it should have shut down long ago. He could never withstand the operation. They were very sorry, but Samuel was dying. How much time did he have? No one knew, maybe a few days. They encouraged us to spend as much time as we could with him. They would help us hold him amid all the wires and tubes. They were very sorry. For them, that was the end of it. For us, it was the beginning. We were not giving up. Samuel was unable to fight for himself, so his parents and grandparents fought day and night for someone to give Samuel a chance.

The social worker took us into her office after the meeting and suggested that we begin to make funeral arrangements. We were horrified—funeral arrangements! I cannot begin to tell you all the emotions that flooded us. We were numb, unable to formulate any plans. We all agreed on one thing however: We refused to stand by while they let our son/grandson slip away from us.

The four of us prayed and talked. We decided to ask the doctors if we could meet with them again. Tom and Marie asked if they would reconsider and please put Samuel on the waiting list for a liver. They flatly refused. They gently but firmly told us that Samuel wouldn't live long enough to get a liver. Secondly, if by a miracle he did, they wouldn't waste a liver on him because he had almost no chance to survive. They would give it to one of the many people already on the waiting list nationwide that had a good chance of survival. A donor liver would be wasted on Samuel, they said. Our next course of action was to ask them if they would consider doing a live donor. They again gently but firmly said no. A donation of part of the liver from a liver donor was dangerous, and it wasn't worth the risk to the donor because Samuel wasn't going to make it. David then spoke up and said that he wanted to be a liver donor for Samuel. He knew it was a serious decision, but he had made up his mind. The doctors told him that it was very generous of him, but they refused to accept this. Through tears, my daughter told these doctors that she would obtain a lawyer if she had to because she wasn't going to stand by and watch her son die. They told her she was welcome to try to find doctors that would take the risk of doing a live donor, but he assured us we wouldn't find any because most doctors won't do it even if the chance of survival is excellent. Most doctors feel it is far too risky to chance this type of operation.

Again, the social worker encouraged us to face the facts and do a reality check. We were more than welcome to use her phone to call family and to make arrangements for his funeral.

During the next few days, we called many families and friends and asked for prayers for Samuel.

A close friend of ours, Fr. John, offered to come to Massachusetts General Hospital and confirm Samuel and to pray with him. He came with another couple one evening. Fr. John asked Tom and Marie if it was their choice to have Samuel confirmed in the Catholic faith. They said yes. They were asked what name they chose for Samuel's confirmation name. They chose Joseph, in honor of St. Joseph who they knew had been helping Samuel by interceding for him. So it was on that night in June that Samuel made his confirmation with his parents, grandparents, two close friends, and Samuel's nurse.

I was in agony watching the suffering of my daughter and son-in-law. I remember one night, I was praying and calling out to God. The prayer that was being formulated in my mind and heart was this: "Father, if you are taking Samuel away from us to be with you, please take him quickly. This child is suffering so much, and Tom and Marie are suffering intensely. I cannot stand to see this suffering any longer." God broke into my thoughts/prayers and asked me who I was to tell Him when to end someone's life or someone's suffering. He told me, in no uncertain terms, that Samuel, and indeed all of us, would suffer for as long as God intended in the way that He wanted because He is God, and I am not! Since then, I only ask for God's mercy on a suffering soul. I leave God free to show that mercy in whatever way He chooses, whether healing, consolation, etc. Who knows, perhaps some souls are lessening their purgatory time by suffering in this way.

Before I continue with the most eventful week of Samuel Thomas Joseph Xiarhos's life, I must do a side step to tell you how marvelously God was providing for all our needs during this time.

As you can well imagine, we had many needs while we were in Boston. Money was becoming a problem. Marie was on maternity leave; I had taken a leave of absence from my job; Dave was retired and receiving a modest pension; and Tom was going to school, running back and forth to the hospital and trying to work a few hours in between. As I mentioned earlier, the hospital staff was very gracious and let the four of us stay in a small room, adjacent to the intensive care unit. The first room they gave us did not have a bathroom. We had to go down the hall and use a common bathroom and shower with many other parents. However, when this small room became vacant with a bathroom, they gave it to us, knowing that we would probably be there for a while. Marie was able to receive a hospital tray at each meal because she was feeding Samuel. (Due to Samuel's inability to nurse, my daughter had to pump her milk every three hours faithfully, twenty-four hours a day.) We used to set the alarm, and she and I would get up every three hours during the night. After she pumped, I would have to mark the container and bring it into the nursery for refrigeration. The hospital staff would then use this milk and put it into Samuel's feeding tube. This went on for almost four months. The staff encouraged Marie to order extra food on her tray to help feed at least one of the rest of us. In the beginning, we brought our cooler from home and kept filling it with ice. We would buy water and soda and juice at a nearby store and put it in there to keep cool. Later on, friends let us borrow a small refrigerator, and we received permission to put it in our tiny room. When we went walking, we often walked near Boston City Hall. We quickly learned (from observing the homeless) that many times during the week, there were people there giving away free samples of food and drink. We were given all sorts of things. One day, they were giving out yogurt, and we all went to receive one. After the man gave us each one, he reached down and picked up a case of yogurt and gave it to us. Things like this were always happening. Each day we were amazed at how well our Father was taking care of us. We felt so loved by God. A close friend of ours, Fr. Giudice, had told a parishioner about our situation. He gave him a good amount of money and told Father to take the four of us out to dinner. Father drove to the hospital on the Fourth of July, and we walked to a beautiful outdoor restaurant and had a wonderful meal together. That one act of love refreshed and renewed us in a marvelous way.

We had to pay $6 per day per car while we were there, even though we never used the cars. It was getting pretty expensive. Finally, after a couple of months, one of the social workers was able to obtain not one but two passes. We no longer had to pay. This in itself was a small miracle because these passes were hard to come by, and only the parents of the child usually got one.

One time, after we had been there for approximately one month, Marie got very sick and had to be hospitalized. Tom had gone home for a few days to school and work, and Dave had gone home to get a few things done. Marie was admitted to the hospital and put in a room on the seventeenth floor. At the same time, I had a sinus infection and could barely lift my head. They were so kind. They put Marie in a room that had a second bed that was empty, and the hospital staff allowed me to use the bed while Marie was a patient. It felt so good to sleep in a real bed. Each day I would go down to the third floor where Samuel was and stay with him. When he would sleep, then I would go back upstairs to Marie. Another thing that we were all grateful for was that it was springtime and then summer. We were able to get out occasionally and take a walk. If it had been wintertime, traveling would have been difficult. God is so good and even arranged the time of year for this to take place.

Now I will attempt to describe to you what took place the week of June 18–24, 2000.

Sunday, June 18, was Father's Day! It should have been a day for a cookout with all of our family celebrating Tom's first Father's Day! Instead it was a day of intense pain and suffering. We were told that Samuel would probably die this week. They were all amazed that he was still alive. Tom and Marie invited both families to come to the hospital and spend Father's Day with Samuel. The hospital staff reluctantly allowed us to use a room adjacent to the cafeteria so that all of us could be together. (They didn't want Samuel out of intensive care.) Tom's parents and two brothers came. My parents came, and my sister and brother-in-law and their three children came. Samuel made his grand entrance with all sorts of tubes and wires connected to him. He was alert, and we took many pictures. We wanted to remember this day. The day was filled with a heaviness as each member of our family left, knowing that they probably would never see Samuel again.

Father's Day, four generations

I believe that it was Tuesday, June 20, that Samuel took a turn for the worse. He was beginning to bleed internally and was slipping into a coma (just what the doctors suspected would happen). It was six o'clock in the morning, and the nurse on duty advised Tom not to leave for school that morning because she was pretty sure it was only a matter of a few hours now. We took turns lying in a bed with Samuel in our arms, talking to him, and releasing him to God. We again made phone calls and asked for emergency prayers. We just sat and prayed and waited with Samuel. At approximately twelve noon, Samuel opened his eyes. The nurse on duty could hardly believe this. After he had been examined, it was determined that the bleeding had stopped. We were told not to get our hopes up because it was still just a matter of a few days or less.

The following day, Wednesday, June 21, Dr. Vacanti, the chief liver transplant surgeon, walked through the intensive care unit and stopped at Samuel's crib. Later on, he called Tom and Marie and Dave and me. He said that he thought we might have a window of opportunity for Samuel to have a liver transplant. He said that he didn't really know why he was agreeing to it but that, if Dave was still willing to undergo this serious operation, he would attempt to take a piece of Dave's liver and give it to Samuel. Earlier in the month, Dave had gone through several tests to see if he would be a candidate to be a liver donor just in case the situation arrived. Now I was really nervous. I didn't want to lose my grandson, but I also didn't want to take a chance of losing my husband. Dave was determined to go through with the operation. On Friday, June 23, I told my daughter that I had to go home and be away from the situation so I could think and pray. That night I arrived at my home for the first time since we left on May 3.

I clearly remember standing in my kitchen at ten o'clock that evening and screaming out to God. I told Him that we needed a miracle! I was afraid of losing my husband, but on the other hand, I couldn't stand by and watch my grandson die. Anyway, Dave was adamant about the operation that had to be done immediately. I went to bed, and as I lay there trying to sleep, the phone rang. I was fearful that it was Marie with bad news. I was right, it was Marie, but she had good news for us. She told us that we had to get right back to the hospital. A young woman had just died in Connecticut, and the hospital staff had asked the family if they would be willing to donate their daughter's organs. The family mentioned that their daughter had always wanted to get married and have a son. They asked if there was a little boy that they could help. Somehow, Samuel's name came up, and the family agreed to give Samuel their daughter's liver. The transplant team had already left by helicopter to harvest the liver in Waterbury, Connecticut.

We were told that the liver would arrive around 8:00 a.m., and they would have to move quickly. They only had a short period of time to get the new liver into Samuel. Eight o'clock came and went and no liver and no word. I prayed and sensed that one of the family members was changing their mind about the organ dona-tion. I prayed and prayed and finally my peace returned. I felt that the situation had been resolved. A couple of hours later, the doctors arrived with the liver. (One year later, I found out that at that precise moment, the mother of this young woman was having second thoughts about this decision.) A team of doctors and nurses came in to see us. They told us that Samuel's chances of survival were not very good. His lungs could collapse, his heart might stop beating, and many, many other situations might occur because his organs had been badly compromised. The operation would take approximately twenty-two hours, and they would try to give us an update every few hours. They looked at Tom and Marie and told them that their child would probably die on the operating table. Were they sure they wanted to go ahead with the transplant? Tom and Marie barely could get the words out, but they both said "yes." Then the nurse took a picture of each of us holding a very yellow Samuel (with a Polaroid camera) and gave it to us to hold while he was in the operating room. We all kissed Samuel, and he was whisked off! Dr. Vacanti stayed back for a moment and turned to us and said, "I'm an excellent surgeon. I can take any liver and shave it down and make it fit. However, only GOD can make it work. *Pray!*" Dr. Vacanti again asked if they were absolutely sure about their decision.

After twelve hours in surgery, the team of four transplant doctors came to speak with us: Samuel had made it! He had beaten all odds! The operation took only twelve hours instead of the anticipated twenty-two. The doctor said that, as soon as he connected the new liver into Samuel's body, it pinked up right away. He said it was truly amazing! None of the situations they thought might happen, occurred. The transplant was done without incident (in itself a miracle). Another miracle: When the doctors finally got a firsthand look at Samuel's diseased liver, they didn't know how he had lived with it for two months.

However, we were not out of the woods yet. We still had a long way to go. Samuel was intubated, and they could not get him off the respirator. Many times, with his tiny hands, Samuel would self-extubate, and the doctors would have to reintubate him over and over again. All this time, we wore masks and gowns and watched with the doctors for any sign of Samuel's body rejecting his new liver. Along with all this came many, many types of medicines that Samuel would have to take to keep his body from rejecting this new organ. One day Samuel would appear to be making progress; the next day it appeared he had taken two steps backward. This roller-coaster ride went on for two months. This was a time for further trusting, more prayer, and lessons in perseverance. In August, the doctors began to be very concerned that Samuel may never be able to come off the respirator. They talked of a tracheotomy. All sorts of questions kept coming from the doctors and from the four of us with no answers! How could we take Samuel home if he was on a respirator? How long could he stay in the hospital on a respirator? We wanted him off the feeding tube, but it looked hopeless. Could we take Samuel home with a feeding tube? The doctors weren't very optimistic. We had to do a reality check. Could Tom and Marie care for Samuel at home? Was this possible? Had we come this far only to find ourselves at a dead end? More lessons. This time we learned about hope. Jesus showed us how to keep hope alive in our hearts. He showed us that there is always reason to hope because nothing is impossible for God! Every day a new set of problems arose, and every day God sustained us. We learned firsthand about the scripture passage that says, "Don't worry about tomorrow. Today has enough problems of its own." How true that was for us! We didn't even have the strength or energy to think about what problems might happen tomorrow; we were focused on the moment!

Finally, the day and moment came! Samuel would finally leave Massachusetts General Hospital on August 22, 2000 (the Feast of the Queenship of Mary) after spending the first four months of his life in a hospital. Dave and I went home on August 21 so that Tom and Marie could be alone to take their son home. Samuel had to come home with a feeding tube and with oxygen. He had to have nurses come to the house and sit with him while he slept at night. But he made it! On the Feast of the Queenship of Mary, Samuel Thomas Joseph Xiarhos finally entered the world outside the hospital on a warm August morning.

At last, this ordeal was coming to an end, or so we thought. We were soon to learn that this was just the beginning!

The following is something I read in a book. I believe it most accurately sums up what God did in my soul during these four months of suffering.

It is this infinitely loving God who, after freeing me from the slavery of sin, has given me the incomparable grace of my vocation and has mysteriously attracted me into the enclosed garden of His delights. This God who is my Savior has made Himself my bridegroom. Alleluia!

CONTINUATION OF THE JOURNEY

If you have read the introductory chapter, you will readily see that I thought this painful ordeal was over after four grueling and challenging months. Boy, was I wrong!

Samuel was home, but the trials were really just beginning. He had a feeding tube and a mask to help him breathe. Nurses had to be hired to stay by Samuel's little crib so his parents could sleep. This went on for over a month. Then Samuel seemed to be doing better and actually seemed to be thriving a bit. Although he was baptized in the hospital, Fr. Giudice did a formal ceremony at the cathedral of St. Peter and St. Paul. So many people that had prayed for Samuel wanted to attend this celebration. Father graciously offered us the basement of the church for a rather large gathering.

Over one hundred people attended. Life was good. However, the next day, Samuel became very ill and was rushed back to Massachusetts General Hospital and was admitted. After a week or so, he was allowed to return home. Life was good again, or so we thought. He returned to the hospital every week for a checkup, and occasionally, he had to be admitted.

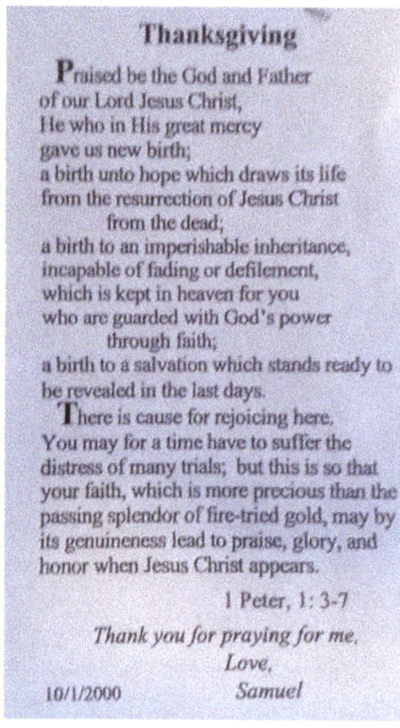

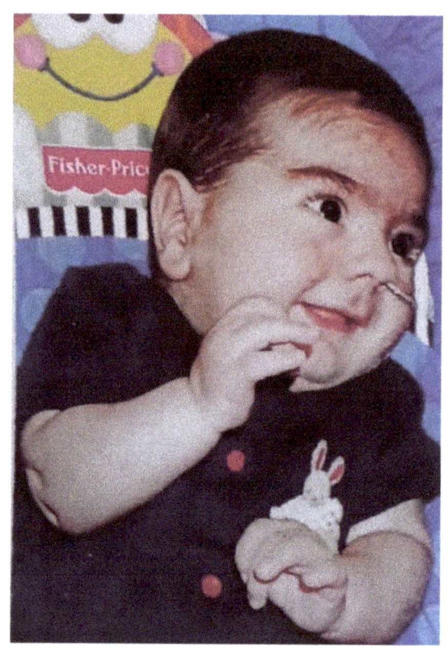

Let's Celebrate!

Now that I'm better, we're going to have a *party*!

We are going to celebrate the sacrament of baptism and confirmation that I received in the hospital!

WHO?   ME!
              SAMUEL THOMAS JOSEPH XIARHOS

WHERE?   THE CATHEDRAL OF SAINTS
                       PETER & PAUL
                       30 FENNER STREET
                       PROVIDENCE, RI

WHEN?   SUNDAY, OCTOBER 1, 2000
2:00 P.M.

We will have a party downstairs in the church hall after the ceremony. Mommy told me that there is going to be lots of delicious food! Please call my mommy by Wednesday. September 27 to tell her you will come (822-4019). I want to meet you and thank you in person for praying for me. See you soon and God bless you.

PS: Please continue to pray for me. I am still on oxygen and would really like to get this tube out of my nose.

Hi,

Allow me to introduce myself. For those of you who don't know me, I am Samuel.

I was born on April 24, 2000, at 10:24 p.m. I weighed 8 lbs., 2 oz., and I was named Samuel Thomas Xiarhos.

About 1 1/2 hours after I was born, I had difficulty breathing, so the doctor put me on a respirator to help me breathe. I was very critical. On April 26, I was baptized at Woman & Infants Hospital by Fr. Francis Guidice. My godparents are Marie Issa (my great-auntie) and George Xiarhos (my uncle).

On May 5, I was transferred to Massachusetts General Hospital in Boston. The doctors did surgery and put me on an ECMO machine, which went into my jugular vein, to try to save my life. I didn't do too well on it though. A few hours later, they had to do more surgery and connect me to the ECMO through my jugular and carotid artery. I did much better on that. I was on that almost three weeks. I came off just in time for mommy's birthday! On May 27, she held me for the first time since I was born. Boy, it sure was worth waiting for. Now I want her to hold me all the time!

I was very jaundiced. (That means something different to grown-ups. To me, it means I was very yellow.) The doctors at Massachusetts

General took lots of tests and found out that my liver was destroyed, and they said I had neonatal hemochromatosis. (That is a grown-up word for "too much iron and scarring in my liver.") I don't know how to say that yet, but daddy will teach me when I get bigger. The doctors said I needed a new liver, or I would die. But I was too sick to have the operation. Daddy and mommy prayed. And all of you did too. I got worse and became very critical. Fr. John Dreher came all the way up to Boston. I was given the sacrament of confirmation by Fr. John on June 19, 2000. My dad and mom gave me the name Joseph as my confirmation name. They had been praying a lot to St. Joseph to intercede for my healing. Every day they rubbed me with holy oil that came all the way from St. Joseph's Oratory in Canada! Daddy and mommy are going to take me there next year in Thanksgiving for his intercession. (They will tell me what that means when I get bigger.) Grandpa, Grandma, Richard, and Kathy Brissette were all at my confirmation. My sponsor was my grandpa.

For the next two days, I got much worse and started to slip into a coma. Mommy and daddy were very sad. Many, many people were praying. Then God did another miracle; I opened my eyes and began feeling much better. But I still needed a new liver. Grandpa decided to give me part of his liver, but God had another plan. On my second-month birthday (June 24), I received a piece of a liver from a little girl who died in Connecticut. (Please pray for her family too.) I was very good during my twelve-hour operation and didn't give the doctors or nurses any trouble. I really like my new liver and am doing quite well.

I finally left the hospital at four months old and came to my home and my own crib on August 22 (the Feast of the Queenship of Mary—I love her so much because my mommy is named after her).

Thanks to my daddy and mommy and all of you who prayed for me; I am doing well and adjusting to my home and the outside world.

*****

Once when Samuel seemed to be doing well, we were given permission to bring him out with us to a restaurant. We had to be extremely careful taking him out anywhere due to his immune system being compromised by his liver transplant. We had not been out in almost a year. We went to a very nice place and ordered our meals as we watched Samuel in his carrier. All of a sudden, Samuel turned a bad color and seemed to be having difficulty breathing. We left immediately and drove to Hasbro Children's Hospital. Marie and I and Samuel rushed into the hospital while Dave and Tom parked the car.

While we were in the examining room, Marie chose at that most inopportune moment to tell me that she was pregnant again. This child would be born in August (approximately four months after Samuel would turn one).

One day, Dr. Vacanti was going to be speaking to many doctors from all over the country. Dave and I were in an auditorium at MGH. The doctor explained about Samuel's liver and showed pictures of it. Even I could tell how destroyed it looked. The doctors asked many questions, and then one of them asked how old he was when He died. At that moment, he had Marie holding Samuel come onto the stage. You should have heard the doctors. Not one of them could believe that Samuel was alive and thriving. They all came to look at him. Samuel had made medical history for many reasons.

When there is a donor transplant, it is almost always done anonymously through the donor bank. The donor family has no idea who is being given the organ, and the organ recipient and family have no idea where this organ came from.

When Samuel was approximately nine months old, my daughter received a letter stating that the donor family would like to meet Samuel. They felt that part of their beautiful daughter, Nicolina, was still alive in Samuel. This beautiful Italian family lived in Waterbury, Connecticut (approximately two hours away). They had made a beautiful flower garden dedicated to Nicolina, who died and whose liver was in Samuel.

Immediately, we all agreed we wanted to meet this most gracious family. We were so grateful to them. we were excited to meet them, thank them, and have them meet Samuel. So on a beautiful sunny Sunday morning, we drove to Connecticut. (Marie was pregnant with Stephen.) When we arrived, we were greeted by the entire family, including all aunts and uncles. Well, Tom and Marie chose to have Samuel learn to call them Grandpa Tony and Grandma Lucy and Auntie Maria. Let me tell you how blessed Samuel was to have three sets of grandparents who loved him so very much and an auntie Maria who loved him so very much. We have had many cookouts with them. Tony and Lucy are fabulous Italian cooks. When Marie delivered her third child and first daughter (Katrina Marie), Auntie Maria was asked to be her godmother. How exciting! Now we were really connected! Twenty-two years later, and we are all a close family. Samuel still has his grandpa Tony, grandma,

Grandpa Tony and Grandma Lucy (holding Samuel) and Auntie Maria

Lucy, and auntie Maria to cheer him along. Praise God!

Now that she was pregnant again, their little apartment would be too small for the four of them. Through the grace of God (and a little help from us), they were able to build a small home in Warwick. While their home was being built, the three of them came to live with Dave and I for a few months. Tom had secured a job at Miriam Hospital as a respiratory therapist, and Marie was studying to pass her nursing boards.

Finally, just before Stephen was to be born, they were able to move into their new home. Then the morning of August 20 came.

(Marie had to deliver her children by Cesarean section.) We left Samuel with Grandpa, while Tom and I took Marie to the hospital. Due to the section, only Tom was allowed in the delivery room with her. However, just as they did when Samuel was born, they put a chair right outside the delivery room for me to sit and say my rosary. I waited and waited, wondering what could be taking so long. Tom was supposed to bring out Stephen Thomas and place him in my arms. All of a sudden, I saw two nurses and a doctor rush into the delivery room. My heart sank. This could not be for Stephen. It absolutely could not! However, when they came out, my little Stephen was there, being rushed into intensive care. I almost passed out. How could this be? Finally, Tom came out and said it was just a precaution because of Samuel's history. Shortly later, the doctor came to see the three of us and said, after examining Stephen, it appeared he may have the same problem as Samuel. He was demonstrating the same problems that Samuel had shortly after his birth. So once again on the second day, we were advised to get a priest in to baptize Stephen. Fr. Giudice came right away and baptized him. We were numb and in shock. On the third day, Tom and Marie decided not to wait any longer. They wanted Stephen at Massachusetts General Hospital right away. They called Dr. Reddy (who was on call that evening) and told him they wanted their son transferred immediately that same night. He had no choice but to allow him to be transferred. The hospital told Marie that she could not go with him because she was not ready to be discharged. Her exact words were "watch me." She signed herself out against doctor's orders, and she and Tom followed the ambulance to Boston. Dr. Reddy carried Stephen in his arms in the ambulance. This time, I could not go with them because Dave and I had to care for Samuel who was now almost sixteen months old.

The doctors at Massachusetts General Hospital thought that Stephen might have to go on an ECMO machine as did Samuel. Once again, the hospital was so good and gave Tom and Marie a tiny room. God is so good and so faithful. Tom and Marie's faith was being severely tested. But once again, God used it to strengthen them.

Miraculously, Stephen did not need to go on ECMO. He was diagnosed with PPHN (persistent pulmonary hypertension of the newborn). He was treated and allowed to come home on September 10 (one day before the terrorist attack). The three of them came straight to our home. We laid him in the living room. He was approximately two weeks old. He came home with a feeding tube. While we were having lunch with Samuel, I peeked in and saw that his little hands had pulled the feeding tube out. Obviously, he didn't need it and was trying to tell us so. From that time on, he ate and drank like any other baby (praise God).

They were now in their new home and adjusting to two babies. Samuel continued to have different medical issues and spent a lot of time back and forth to Massachusetts General Hospital while grandpa and I cared for Stephen. While we were constantly on the alert for health issues, a new concern started to arise. Samuel was very late crawling, walking, and getting toilet trained. He also was very late speaking. One day, when we were at the table with friends, he kept saying "hi" to them over and over again. This may not seem like much, but it triggered something in me, and I asked Marie if she thought we should get him some type of testing. He was also flapping his hands near his mouth. After extensive testing, Tom, Marie, and I went (on Tom's birthday) to get the results. We were told that Samuel was autistic. He had Asperger's. We all nearly fainted in the office. There had to be some mistake. However, as time went on, it was clear that they had made the correct diagnosis. Now he had health problems *and* autism. How were we supposed to handle both of these problems and care for Stephen? Well, we learned rather quickly that God gives the graces we need at the moment we need them and not a minute before. We began to read all we could on autism. We were taking baby steps toward accepting this and trying to lead normal lives.

One night, I had a dream that my two daughters-in-law and my daughter were all pregnant at the same time. When I awoke, I laughed because it appeared that Chris and Elena would not be able to have children as they had been trying for many years. Matthew and

Teresa had two girls who were approximately six and eight years old at the time of the dream. Tom and Marie certainly had their hands full with their boys. A few months later, Dave and I went to Florida to visit our sons and their families. While we were there, Matthew and Teresa told us they were expecting again. We were thrilled for them but felt so sad for Chris and Elena. Around that time, Dave and I were preparing to go on a pilgrimage to Fatima, Portugal, with our very dear friend, Fr. John Dreher. However, as the time drew closer to the departure date, I felt I didn't want to go. I hated to be away from Marie for that long because one never knew what could happen from one moment to the next. One day, I shared this feeling with two religious sisters that I was very close with. They had both been to Our Lady of Fatima Shrine in Portugal and encouraged us to indeed go on this beautiful pilgrimage. They suggested that we offer the trip up to Almighty God for a pregnancy for Elena. That is exactly what we did.

Shortly after we returned from our pilgrimage, we went back down to Florida to visit our sons. On Sunday, Chris and Elena and Dave and I went to Sacred Heart Church in downtown Tampa for Mass. The scripture reading for that Sunday said, "This time next year, you will have a son." My heart jumped inside me, and I felt those words were meant for Elena that day. On the flight home, I kept thinking that she might be pregnant. Sometime after our return home, Chris called me at work. He said that he knew we always came down to Florida in February, but would we mind coming in March next year, and could we arrange to stay for three weeks? And then, while crying, he told me that Elena was pregnant and due in March. How good our God is! How faithful He is. He will *never* be outdone in generosity. Boy, was I glad we went on our pilgrimage to Fatima.

I decided to give Elena a baby shower in Rhode Island in November so that family and friends could all celebrate with her. By the way, sometime before they came up to Rhode Island, the sonogram confirmed that she was having twins! Elena herself is a twin. The next sonogram confirmed that she was having a boy and a girl!

(I should mention here that many years ago, while in church, God had shown me that my seventh grandchild would be a boy and would serve Him in a very special way.) I received this and confirmation of it many, many times. I already had five grandchildren. The twins would be my sixth and seventh. So I knew that their daughter would be delivered first and their son, second, as he would be my seventh grandchild. Meanwhile, Chris asked the doctor how he would determine which child would be delivered first. The doctor told him that whichever one he could reach first would be delivered first. I told Chris that Chloe would be first, and Kyle Christopher would be second.

He laughed and said, "Mom, even the doctor doesn't know."

I said, "Watch and see." And of course, by now I am sure you have guessed that Kyle Christopher became my seventh grandchild!

Now getting back to the baby shower for Elena, we had a wonderful time celebrating the goodness of God to Chris and Elena. She received many beautiful and necessary items for the twins. Later that evening, my daughter told us that she was pregnant with her third child. (Remember my dream?) Yes, all three were pregnant at the same time. (Praise God!) Teresa gave birth to their first son, Peter Matthew, on Nov 26, 2002. Elena was due in March but gave birth to two small but very healthy babies on February 20, 2003. When I called our friends—the sisters—that evening to share the good news, they told me that February 20 was the feast day of Francesco and his sister, Jacinta. These were two of the children Our Lady appeared to in Fatima, Portugal. Remember our pilgrimage? Coincidence? No, I think *not*! Dave and I stayed in Florida three weeks, helping care for the twins. Meanwhile, Samuel was in Rhode Island and actually behaving himself and staying out of the hospital! Thank you, Father! Marie went into the hospital on June 30 to deliver her

Jacinta and Francisco

daughter. Grandpa stayed home with Samuel and Stephen, while Tom and I went with Marie to the hospital. Again, a chair was put outside the delivery room for me to say my rosary. Shortly, Tom came out and put a very healthy and beautiful Katrina Marie in my arms. So within approximately seven months, we were blessed with four grandchildren. Thank you, Father!

Now back to Samuel's story (or so it seems). Tom and Marie's small home in Warwick was getting a bit crowded but still manageable. Dave decided to make a beautiful large family room for them in their basement. Dave, being a perfectionist, did a rather outstanding job. It was such a blessing because there was so much room for the three little ones to play. Tom and Marie put a small television down there for the children to watch movies on occasion. Dave also built them a large deck on which we enjoyed many cookouts.

On April 2, 2005, the world mourned the death of our beloved John Paul II. The Sunday after his death, Marie was trying the get the three children ready for Mass at St. Matthew's Church in Cranston. Tom and Katrina and Stephen were already in the car. Marie noticed that Samuel (almost five) was talking to someone, but no one was there. This troubled her. So she asked him who he was speaking with. He said John Paul and Jesus. Marie asked him if he meant Fr. John, our dear friend. He said no, that he was speaking to John Paul. Marie asked him what they were discussing. He told her that John Paul told him not to be afraid because Jesus and he were going to fix him. Marie didn't know what to make of this. She quickly got Samuel in the car, and off to Mass they went. That particular Sunday, every church in our diocese had a picture of John Paul II on the altar. When Marie walked into church, holding Samuel's hand, he shouted, "Mom, there's John Paul!" She was shocked because there was no way he could have known this. They did not have a picture of him in their home he didn't go to school, and he didn't watch TV. She asked him how he knew that, and he looked at her and said, "I told you I was just speaking with him." That Sunday evening, while I was rocking him before bed, he told me the same thing. I did not ask him any questions, and he didn't elaborate any further.

A few weeks later, Samuel was once again rushed to Massachusetts General Hospital. After many tests, the doctors agreed that he needed to have his spleen removed due to enlargement of the spleen. The day came, and we waited and prayed. He came through it okay. The next day, he told us that John Paul was with him during the surgery and told him not to be afraid. He was going to help him. Two or three other times, he casually mentioned that John Paul was with him during surgery, but he never elaborated.

I forgot to mention something. Approximately one week after he saw John Paul's picture in church, he had a sleepover at our home. On the way back to his home in Warwick, he told me that he was going to have to go to the hospital that evening. I explained to him that he was not sick and did not need to go to the hospital. Three times he told me this, and three times I gave him the same answer. Early evening, Dave and I decided to go out to dinner as we had not been out for quite a while. Of course by now I am sure you have guessed what happened. Yes! As we were eating, Dave received a call that Samuel had been rushed to the hospital. So much for dinner. We rushed over, and while we were in the examining room, he cried out for John Paul. Marie reminded him that John Paul had died. He said, and I quote, "Oh, that's right, we have a new pope and his name is Benedict." Pope Benedict had been elected the day before. The nurse looked at us and asked if this was true. Of course, once again, there was no way that Samuel could have known this.

During this time, Dave and I were getting pretty fatigued running back and forth from Providence to Warwick—sometimes in heavy traffic, sometimes in the middle of the night. Marie had passed her nursing boards and had secured a position at Woman & Infants Hospital. She is such a wonderful holy nurse. She has experienced the birth of sick children as well as a healthy ones. She can sympathize and help women because she has had so many near-death experiences with her own children.

Tom worked at Miriam Hospital on the 3:00–11:00 shift, and Marie worked three nights, 3:00–11:00. Therefore we babysat in Warwick till 11:30 p.m. or midnight. Between this schedule and running back and forth for emergencies, our health became compromised.

We began conversations that maybe we should all live together so when Samuel gets rushed to the hospital, we would be right there and try to keep the other two children's lives as normal as possible without Dad and Mom in the home.

We thought that perhaps in four or five years we may consider looking for a home for all of us to live. David and I totally enjoyed our home in Providence with nine rooms, a cedar closet, a finished basement, and a large deck. We were certainly not ready to leave. Well, it seems that God had a different idea. Through prayer, we discerned that we should start exploring our options. So we began looking at homes that could have a potential of an in-law apartment and within our price range. For the next two years, we spent most Sundays driving by homes and visiting some of them. None was big enough for all seven of us. One Sunday, I took some paper, and the four of us sat down at the table. I asked each one what was important to them in a home that we might buy. I said that if God could give us the perfect home, what would each one ask Him to provide? Tom answered first. He told us how much he dislikes watering the grass and would like a sprinkler system. He also wanted central air-conditioning. Marie was next. She had quite the list! She wanted a huge colonial home with a farmer's porch. She also wanted four bedrooms, a playroom for the children, and a large gas fireplace. Dave's turn: He did not want a septic system. He wanted a sewer system. He wanted to live kind of in the country but not too far away from stores, etc. He also wanted gas heat and not oil and a large shed. *My desires were rather simple*, I thought. I wanted a large enough bedroom that I could put a prayer chair and a small table for my prayer time. I also wanted to be no more than one mile from a Catholic Church in case of storms, etc., and I couldn't get to our own church.

Finally, we found a plat in Smithfield that we could afford and build on. However, long story short, after paying $4,000 for a floor plan for our new home, the builder dissolved his business, and we were left with a $4,000 floor plan that we no longer needed. We were devastated. However, we all consciously made a decision to trust in God and not to get discouraged.

Dave had been looking on the Internet and checking out all sorts of leads. However, nothing panned out, and we began to be emotionally drained. Monday of Holy Week 2005 was a turning point. During my prayer time in the morning, I was increasingly aware of the Lord telling me to stop looking for a home and concentrate on having a truly Holy Week. I felt the Lord telling me that *He* would actually *hand* the home to us so *He* would be glorified. I shared with Dave, and he agreed. We put the computer away and concentrated on the beauty and holiness of the week and the Paschal mystery. (I was secretly beginning to think that we were searching for something that was impossible.) Good Friday, I picked up my dad to bring him to a doctor's appointment. When I arrived at their home to get him, my mom handed me a piece of newspaper and said that she thought this was the house God wanted us to live in and that she was supposed to "hand" this paper to me. I took it and kind of chuckled to myself. We had been searching for over two years, and my mom thought this was it? While I waited for my dad at the doctor's office, I took the article out of my purse, read it, and then put it back. I think I did this three times. By the time I brought my dad home, I was very excited. I called Dave and asked him to meet me at my parents' home and told him about the house my mom found. Dave also chuckled. However, he did come, and we took my parents and did a ride by to see it. We were cautiously optimistic and wondered if this could really be it. The article said that they were having open house the following Sunday. I was disappointed because that was Mercy Sunday and we would be in church during the time of the open house. My dad encouraged me to call and see if we could go see it that evening. I wasn't sure if we should be doing this on Good Friday, but I did call. The wife answered and said she would have to call her husband and ask him. She assured me that she would call me back. A short time later, she called and said it would be fine for us to come that evening. We took Stephen with us. As we entered North Smithfield (we had been looking at the other end of the state), I asked the Lord to please give us a clear sign if this was indeed the one that He had picked out for us. I told God that if they were Christian, then I would believe this house was a gift to us from Him.

The family was very gracious to us. They had three children and were moving back to Michigan where the wife's family lived. He was a builder and had built this house himself. It was built in 2000, and they moved into this home in May of 2000. That was less than two weeks after Samuel was born! We spent a long time with them. At one point, the mother served dinner to her children. She served them *meat*! I was devastated because it was beginning to appear this indeed might be the home, but they were eating meat on Good Friday! Suddenly I remembered that I had asked the Lord that they be a Christian family, not necessarily a Catholic family. We soon discovered that they were Baptists and loved our Lord God very much. Whew! We asked if Tom and Marie could come with us the next day to see it. They agreed.

When we arrived the next morning, they met us very excitedly and told us that God had revealed to them that this house was meant for us. They immediately took $20,000 off the price. They told us that somehow they knew they had to make this work for us. Someone had offered them more money the week before, and for some unknown reason, they decided to refuse. Now we were starting to get excited. Dave did a little research. He found that almost all of North Smithfield had a septic tank and had oil for heating. To our great surprise, this little cul-de-sac had sewer, not septic, and had gas and not oil. We also had a wonderful well for our water. We were kind of in the country, nice and quiet, with a horse farm bordering our backyard. We were close to shops, etc., though. Tom got excited because it had a huge sprinkler system and six zones of central air-conditioning. Marie got excited because it was a large colonial with a farmer's porch. It also had a large gas fireplace in the living room. Upstairs she had four bedrooms. She also had three bathrooms. The only thing it didn't have was a playroom for the children (which she wanted off the kitchen). Watch and see how God in His mercy provided for that. Mine was easy. We made our bedroom large enough that I had plenty of room for a prayer corner. I took a ride to the nearest Catholic Church, and guess what, it is exactly one mile from our home. It is not our parish but has been very helpful when we had to walk to Mass in snowstorms, etc.

We signed the agreement in April 2005. Dave and I put a lot of money into the house and left only a little for an addition to be constructed for us. The man who sold us the house was going to build our addition, and he told us that he would make it work with the money we had. He most certainly did this and with many extras!

So here we were. God literally "handed" us the house using my mom as his instrument in handing me the newspaper article. Well now came the big challenge of selling both our homes and closing on them. So I began praying. I asked the Blessed Mother to sell both our homes in the month of May, Mary's month. I felt assured by our Blessed Mother that she would see that this took place. Pentecost Sunday in May came. We were having our first open house that afternoon. During my prayer time in the morning, I felt the Holy Spirit instructing me to tell our realtor (a close friend) that, if anyone bought the house this day, we would give them a "Pentecost special" and deduct $20,000 from the selling price. My friend balked at the idea, telling me that some people may not even know what Pentecost is. I told her that was fine because that would give her a chance to witness to them. She finally agreed. Meanwhile, I had asked my spiritual director where Dave and I could go for Pentecost Mass. He suggested St. Theresa Church and Shrine in Harrisville. We had never heard of it. He told us to go straight up Route 7, and we would come to it. So off we went on a beautiful May morning. Literally, as we started up the hill to this country church on Dion Drive (which is my mom's maiden name), Dave and I both experienced the rush of the Holy Spirit upon us, and we knew this was home. This was to become our new parish. We hadn't met any of the parishioners nor the pastor, but we knew God had led us to our new spiritual home just as he had led us to our physical home. We attended a very beautiful and holy Pentecost Mass. After Mass, we introduced ourselves to the pastor and explained how Fr. John Dreher recommended that we spend Pentecost here. We also told him we knew this was our new church home. He did not know what to make of all this. Seventeen years later, and we are very good friends with Fr. Jerry Caron. He is a holy pastor who truly feeds his sheep. Later that evening, approximately 8:30 p.m., our realtor friend called to tell us that our home had been sold, and they were given the Pentecost special and were delighted. Wow! That was fast! Now Tom and Marie had to sell their home in Warwick. Toward the very end of May, we received word that their home, too, had been sold. Thank you, Mother Mary, for your intercession.

Now comes the closing. I started praying to the Most Sacred Heart of Jesus that both homes would close in June in the month dedicated to His most Sacred Heart. Dave and I have great devotion to the Sacred Heart of Jesus and have consecrated our home to His merciful heart. Tom and Marie had also consecrated their home to His heart. My friend told me that this was nearly impossible to close that quickly and on both homes. Well, Jesus will never be outdone in generosity. June 30 was Katrina's second birthday. We celebrated by closing on both our homes. Yes, you heard me correctly. My friend came to the closing on our home in Providence and then had to quickly get to Warwick to close on Tom and Marie's home. Miracle of miracles!

Next problem: We both had to be out of our homes the next day, July 1. However, we had no place to go. The owners of the home we were buying never imagined that we could sell and close so quickly. They were not ready to leave. We had to store our furniture in their garage, and Tom and Marie had to put their furniture in storage for a week. Tom and Marie and their three small children went to stay with friends for that week. David and I stayed with friends in Providence for a few days and then went to stay with friends in Narragansett for the rest of the week. We finally moved into our new home on the morning of July 8. Dave and I had given and sold much of our furniture because we would be living in a much smaller home. We lived in a small bedroom upstairs until after Thanksgiving of that year. We actually lived out of a box. As the weather got colder, we had to try to find our warmer clothes that were buried in the garage somewhere.

During this time, the builder was busy at work. One day, the builder came to us and said he didn't like the way the house looked from the outside. He felt it needed something. He asked Marie if it would be okay if he built a large family room right off the kitchen. He would need to move the deck in order to do this. He said he would just charge for the materials and not for his labor. He had no way of knowing that this was the one thing that Marie wanted so badly. Coincidence? No! Holy Spirit? *Yes*! He even put in two book-cases. It was so beautiful, and he put in wall-to-wall carpeting. What a tremendous gift!

Again, I repeat, God will never be outdone. He loves to surprise His people. He has so much for all of us if we will just trust Him. The following month, August, we received some very unexpected but exciting news. Marie was expecting again! Thank God that our home would be completed before the end of the year. Philip Thomas was to be born in March of 2006. Tom and Marie needed that bed-room now. Katrina was moved into that room, and the room she had been in was turned into a nursery.

September of that year was very memorable. Marie had applied to the Make-A-Wish Foundation for Samuel. They sent all seven of us to Children's Village in Florida for Make-A-Wish recipients and their families. They even offered to pay for Dave and I all the expenses!—airfare for all of us plus a week at a rental home on their property and tickets daily to all the four Disney theme parks. They gave us a rental car, movie camera with discs that they developed for us, and extra cash for souvenirs. It was so beautiful! We got to go on all the rides first because of Samuel—no waiting in lines for us! What a blessing. The kids had horseback riding, miniature golf, a game room, and many other amenities. All our meals were in the main dining room with other families that were staying at Children's Village. The meals were delicious, and there was something for everyone. There was a pizza restaurant on the grounds. We could order any type of pizza anytime we wanted and as many as we wanted. The first day that we arrived, Matthew and family and Chris and family surprised us and met us at the airport. They followed us to the village and spent the entire day with us. We rode the carousel, played miniature golf, visited the game room, and ordered several pizzas. What a day it was! Another surprise from God to His children.

The morning of March 9, 2006, arrived. We left Samuel (almost six), Stephen (four and a half), and Katrina (not quite three) in the capable care of Grandpa. Tom, Marie, and I went off to the hospital once again. And once again, I sat in my chair outside the delivery room, praying the rosary. This time, Tom came out with his son, Philip Thomas, and placed him in my arms. Everyone was delighted. I went home to get Grandpa and the other children, and we all went to visit Mom and their baby brother. All was going well until that evening. Marie had requested that she keep Philip in her room with her. At one point, Philip looked as if he were in distress. Tom called the nurse. After examining him and then calling the doctor, they told Tom and Marie that one of his lungs had collapsed. The doctor wanted Philip to be brought to the nursery. Marie was so hysterical and adamant that her son stayed with her, that they finally relented. The doctor and nurses kept careful watch on baby Philip. Again, another miracle! His lung repaired itself, and he went home with Mom a few days later.

Between March 2006 and March of 2008, Samuel was admitted to the hospital in Boston many more times. Some of these admissions included esophageal varices (we came very close to losing him with this diagnosis), GI bleeds, and encephalopathy. Other admissions were for pneumonia, etc. Shortly before his seventh birthday, he had to have a shunt put into his liver. However, as time went on, the shunt was malfunctioning often and caused his ammonia levels to rise sharply. On his seventh birthday, we had a birthday party for him in our church hall. I had prayer cards made to give out to everyone who came. On one side of the card was a picture of John Paul II (Samuel's hero), and the other side was a current picture of him and a prayer for his healing.

Prayer Request

Samuel Xiarhos had a liver transplant at 2 months old. Now, a beautiful young boy of 7, he needs a miracle to widen the portal vein of his liver or be at risk for damage to his brain (due to his shunt) for the rest of his life. Seemingly, by heavenly intervention, little Samuel has a special love for John Paul II. If you are so moved, *please pray the following:*

Almighty God and Merciful Father, we believe that You grant many graces through the intercession of Your faithful servant, John Paul II. We come to You now, asking through John Paul II's intercession for a widening in the portal vein of Samuel's liver, eliminating the need for his shunt. We ask this through Jesus Christ, Your Son and our Lord.

Amen.

October 1, 2000

We handed out these prayer cards to over one hundred people who came to his birthday party.

Prayer cards were also sent to people literally around the country and also outside the country.

At the beginning of March 2008, the transplant team at Massachusetts General Hospital wanted to meet with us. Dave, good grandpa that he is, offered to care for all four children while Tom, Marie, and I drove to Boston. We went into the room rather hesitatingly, not knowing what to expect. The doctors explained that the portal vein in Samuel's liver had closed. While Tom and Marie were taking this news in, I asked how they intended to reopen it. They gently explained that there was no way to reopen it. The only hope for Samuel was to have a second liver transplant. What? This time, however, we had two major problems:

1. Time. Samuel needed a new liver within two or three weeks, or it would be too late. There was no way he could be put on a list and get a liver in this short time.

2. Due to the fact that he was older (almost eight), the new liver would have to be an exact match. When he was a baby, an exact match was not necessary. Now it was indeed necessary.

You can easily imagine how shocked we all were. A second liver transplant? This would be his third liver. How is this possible? Did we go through these eight challenging years only to meet with a dead end? He had barely survived the first one. There were now three additional children to be cared for. So many thoughts went through our heads in less than an hour. The only hope was that an exact match could be found for Samuel, and the operation would have to take place not later than the first week of April. Tom spoke up and asked if he could be tested to see if he would be a match for his son. They agreed. And through another one of God's miracles, Tom was found to be the exact match that Samuel needed. He readily agreed to give his son part of his liver. The doctors explained all the many risks involved. Tom still decided to go through with it. It was the only chance his son had to live.

Now for the next set of problems:

1. Tom would be out of work for some time, and Marie would also be out of work to stay with Samuel in the hospital in Boston. Dave and I would be home, caring for Stephen, six and a half; Katrina, almost five; and Philip, age two.
2. The doctors put Tom through more tests. After careful examination of him, the transplant doctors discovered that Tom had a rare condition called total situs inversus. Basically, this means that his major organs are reversed or mirrored from their normal positions. (This condition is found in 0.015 percent of the population.) So his heart was on the right side of his chest, his liver on the left side. After much discussion, the doctors agreed that they could still do this transplant, but the operation would have to be

done with mirrors. They were a bit concerned because they had never encountered anything like this.

The doctors picked the date of April 2, 2008, to operate. This happened to be the night John Paul had died three years ago.

It was a very apprehensive morning. We were running from Samuel's hospital room to Tom's hospital room. Our son, Chris, flew up from Tampa, Florida, to be with us and wait with us. Well it was a very long wait. After twelve long hours, Tom was wheeled out of the operating room. He was in horrific pain. Next, Samuel came out, and he looked terrible but was sedated. This was turning out to be a nightmare. The doctors told us that the next forty-eight hours were critical for both of them. Once again, we turned to constant prayer. It was a very long night, and we took turns sleeping. The next few days were difficult. Tom and Samuel were on the same floor but on different wings. Marie kept running back and forth between the two rooms. One Sunday, Dave and I brought the other three children to see their parents and Samuel. Just before we left, I noticed that Samuel's right arm was limp. I didn't like what I saw and mentioned it to my daughter who mentioned it to the nurse who was caring for Samuel in ICU. Later that evening, Marie called me and, in a hysterical voice, told me that Samuel had had a stroke. This is why his arm was limp. His whole right side had been affected. He couldn't walk or hold anything. Now we had a new set of problems. The next time that I was able to get to Boston, I went in to see Tom first. He didn't look well. I noticed that he had a red line going up his right arm, and he was in severe pain. I immediately ran to Samuel's room and asked Marie to go take a look. I stayed with Samuel while she went to check on Tom. She called the nurse, and he was diagnosed with a severe case of cellulitis.

Finally, the day came when Samuel was transferred out of ICU into a regular room. However, shortly after that move, he began to have a series of brain bleeds and was back and forth for imaging of his brain.

(We found out a year later that because of the quantity and severity of these brain bleeds, Samuel was now mild to moderately retarded.) Tom and Samuel were in the hospital for approximately six weeks.

At one point, Tom was discharged, but a couple of days later, he was readmitted due to another infection.

Finally, the day came when all three were returning home. However, it was with a heavy heart that we had to place Samuel in a wheelchair. For part of May, all of June, July, and August, I took Samuel two to three times a week for physical therapy. Rhode Island Rehabilitation did a wonderful job. And by the end of therapy, we were able to return the wheelchair as we watched Samuel begin to walk again. However, to this day, his right side is extremely weak. He cannot write or have the strength to ride a bike or to run.

Tom returned to work, and Samuel returned to school. So we all settled down to begin a "normal life"—*wrong*! We finally came to the conclusion that our lives would never be anything that anyone would call normal. Every day we face numerous challenges in this family. Every day God met us where we were and granted us many, many graces to meet these challenges. We were leaning more and more on this Scripture passage, "The mercies of the Lord are renewed each morning, so great is His faithfulness."

In May of 2010, Dave and I went to spend Memorial Day weekend with Chris and Elena and the twins. My daughter's birthday was May 28. I called her from Florida to wish her a happy birthday. She told me she had a very severe headache, and it was affecting her eyesight. I suggested that she go to the urgent care near our home so that they could give her some medicine to help with the pain. Later that evening, she called to tell me that the doctor had sent her for a CT scan, and they discovered that she had a brain tumor. Shortly after we returned home, she underwent emergency surgery one evening. It was affecting her eyesight, and they had to get in to remove the tumor. Tom and I spent the night at the hospital, waiting and praying. Finally, the doctor came out and told us that he was able to remove most of it but not all of it because of the location of the tumor. Tom went in to see her, and then we returned home. (The good news was that the tumor was benign.) During the next couple of weeks, Marie had to have two more surgeries. She kept leaking spinal fluid. One Saturday, I went into ICU at Rhode Island Hospital. I went in to wash Marie's hair and to spend a good part of the day with her. I had difficulty getting to see her as often as I wished because it was summer, and I had all the children to care for. This Saturday, however, Tom and Dave were with the children. As I walked into her room, I noticed that she looked different. She was extremely weak and seemed to be regressing instead of making progress. She was too weak for me to wash her hair. I just sat with her. I had the nurse call the doctor to come examine her. He told me he didn't understand what was happening because she had been doing so well the day before. Well I found out the next day from the doctor that we almost lost her that day. God, however, took pity on all of us, and she began to come around. Praise our God!

However, she was still leaking spinal fluid. It was decided to call in another neurosurgeon whose specialty was putting shunts into brains. The doctors decided Marie was a candidate for this—another long night. This doctor shaved half of Marie's beautiful hair, drilled a hole in her head, and put a shunt in with a valve. When she was finally wheeled into her room where Tom and I were waiting, I didn't even recognize her. A couple of weeks later, as she was recovering, we received a call that Marie had had a mild stroke. "Dear God," I prayed, "will this nightmare never end?" After nine weeks in the hospital, our daughter finally returned home to her family. Basically, she spent most of the summer in the hospital, and I cared for the four children. It was a bit of a challenge because they were out of school for a good part of her hospitalization. I had to find ways to keep them busy. I wasn't sure how I was going to spend time with my daughter in the hospital while I had these children to entertain. Once again, God was to the rescue! My neighbor took it upon herself to call many summer day camps. After she explained our situation, most of them enrolled the three youngest children free of charge or at a very minimal cost. This was a very traumatic time in our family as you can imagine. Even though their mom was now home, she still could not care for them. They were upset with seeing her with almost no hair on her head. (She had the rest of it shaved.) Through the grace and mercy of God, we got through this ordeal. Also, a huge blessing for me was the deliverance of meals to our home on a regular basis for nine weeks from all our dear friends. The day finally came when Marie could return to work.

At the beginning of 2012, Tom had to return to Massachusetts General Hospital for a complication due to the liver donation. He was operated on and within a week was able to return home. During the time of his hospitalization, he received word that his dad had also become hospitalized in Rhode Island. Once home, he and Marie were heading to the hospital on Saturday morning, March 3. Before they actually left, however, Tom received a call that his dad had unexpectedly passed away (it was Tom's birthday)—another mountain to climb. It was the children's first experience of death and of a family member.

The following year, March 2013, we were having a family birthday party for Philip. He was turning seven. It was such a beautiful spring-like day. Tom went outside to play basketball with the children. He fell and fractured his head and had a serious brain bleed. The rescue was called. After one week in the hospital, he was released. However, the doctors told him he needed rest and complete quiet for the healing to take place. Well we knew he wouldn't get any quiet in our household! So it was decided that Tom would recuperate at his mom's home. Approximately two months later, he was able to return home and to work.

I forgot to mention that when Samuel was approximately eleven years old, he began to realize that he was different from other boys his age. He began to see a psychiatrist and a therapist. His behavior was so challenging and unpredictable. At times we would have to restrain him (sometimes for hours). He would strike us or throw and break things on a regular basis. His behavior has certainly taken a toll on the rest of the family but especially affecting his three siblings.

Moving along now to November of 2014, Samuel's physical health was stable up to this point. Tom and Marie were both working, and Dave and I helped care for the children. We were certainly blessed. Thanksgiving Day came around. For forty-five years, I have hosted Thanksgiving for our family, and this year was no exception. My dad and mom came as usual. My dad had Parkinsons's disease and was having some issues with dementia, so we were thrilled that he had decided to come for dinner with my mom. We even got my dad and mom to toast each other and took lots of great pictures. What a truly enjoyable day that was. Four days later, my mom was found unresponsive in her bed. She spent three weeks at Our Lady of Fatima Hospital. Dave and I were able to spend almost every day with her (usually ten to twelve hours). We had great talks, and I was able to help feed her lunch daily. Slowly she slipped into unconsciousness. Again, God, in His mercy, took care of our needs. The doctor and nurses and entire staff took such good care of my mom, and they were so good to Dave and me. We felt loved and cared for, and indeed we were. When the good Lord took her home to Himself on Monday, December 22 at 3:00 p.m., Dave and I were privileged to be at her side, holding her hands. My mom was ninety-four and a half years old. She and my dad had been married for seventy-one and a half years. Now we had to try to explain this to my dad. He seemed to grasp it, and then he didn't. After a couple of months of asking where she was, he stopped talking about her. His dementia was increasing, and his health started to decline. After a two-day stay at RIH, the good Lord took him to Himself on Friday, April 17, at approximately 5:00 p.m. Dave and I had been with him those two precious days. The day he died, our daughter was able to join us at the hospital to pray with my dad and to help him with his passage into eternity. What a privilege it is to be at the bedside of someone you love deeply as they pass from this world to the next. My dad also was ninety-four and a half years old. What a witness my dad and mom have been to all of us. Their love and commitment to each other and to their family were such example and inspiration. (They died within four months of each other.) I would have to be honest in saying that my mom taught me just about everything I know *except* how to live without her. To this day, I miss both of them more than I could ever express.

In November 2015, my daughter was once again hospitalized. They discovered she had a malfunctioning valve in her shunt. Later the doctor told us that this particular valve had been recalled. The doctor operated and tied off her shunt with the hope and prayer that her brain would no longer need it. It was touch and go for almost four months (during which time she was out of work again). She finally had an MRI at the end of February 2016. The MRI showed that the arteries in her brain appeared to be normal, which would mean she no longer needed the shunt—another miracle! She returned to work on Monday, March 7, 2016. Thank You, Father of mercies! We are now in the Jubilee year of mercy. God is really outdoing Himself in small ways as well as large ones. We are so very blessed. As of this writing, we are in the waiting and praying mode for Samuel. He needs a total hip replacement. Due to the prolonged and high levels of prednisone that was used to keep him alive when he was younger, it had now caused necrosis of his hip. However, during this waiting time, we are getting ready to celebrate Samuel's sixteenth birthday! Yes, our journey has been sixteen long but incredibly beautiful and miraculous years. It truly has been a love affair with our God and His mother.

We have concluded that learning to trust God on deeper levels requires deeper levels of suffering. Without trials and sufferings, why would trust be needed? Thank You, Father, for Your purification through the fires of suffering. What an awesome God we have!

In the words of St, Padre Pio, "Pray. Don't worry, and be happy!" God wants our happiness more than we do.

In closing, I can think of no more appropriate way than the words of a familiar song, "Glory and Praise to Our God."

Glory and praise to our God, Who alone gives light to our days. Many are the blessings He bears to those who trust in His ways.

We, the daughters and sons of Him who built the valleys and plains, praise the wonders our God has done in every heart that sings.

In His wisdom, He strengthens us, like gold that's tested in fire. Though the power of sin prevails, our God is there to save.

Every moment of every day, our God is waiting to save, always ready to seek the lost, to answer those who pray.

Glory and praise to our God, Who alone gives light to our days. Many are the blessings He bears to those who trust in His ways. *Amen*!

Well, Samuel turned twenty-two on April 24, 2022 (Mercy Sunday). His health has been stable with the help of his antirejection meds and, of course, God! He survived COVID twice. This is no small miracle when your body is as compromised as Samuel's is.

However, Samuel became aggressive little by little. As he got older, his aggressiveness became much worse. Many times we had to call 911 to protect ourselves and the other children. This broke our hearts. We finally had to agree to at least start talking and praying about the possibility of Samuel living in a group home with other young men.

After meeting with many doctors, social workers, and therapists, we all finally accepted the fact that Samuel could only thrive in a 24-7 environment.

We tried so very hard to have a structured environment here at home, but with work and school schedules, etc., it became impossible. There are not a lot of small group homes for young men such as Samuel. He is smart and has the best memory of anyone I know.

So the social workers began looking for a place with no success. There was talk of even moving him out of state (which we couldn't have allowed). Through a lot of prayer, many tears, and the merciful gaze of God on Samuel and all of us, a miracle came about.

They were opening a new group home with only five young men that could live there. Each would have their own room. Samuel was first on the list! It is a beautiful ranch home and borders a horse farm. The best news? It is a ten-minute ride from our home.

He is now living there and loves it there, although he enjoys coming to our home once a week for dinner and board games with the entire family. He attends all family parties and functions. He loves going to 4:30 Mass on Saturday with his family and then coming home, and all eight of us enjoy dinner together. Samuel likes to go shopping with his mom and is allowed to pick up treats for himself and the other four young men.

Samuel enjoys listening to music (as most young adults do). His aggressiveness is getting under control. He is on a list to get a part-time job that he might enjoy and be good at. That is what we are praying for.

Thanksgiving

*P*raised be the God and Father
of our Lord Jesus Christ,
He who in His great mercy
gave us new birth,
a birth unto hope which draws its life
from the resurrection of Jesus Christ
from the dead,
a birth to an imperishable inheritance,
incapable of fading or defilement,
which is kept in heaven for you
who are guarded with God's power
through faith,
a birth to a salvation which stands ready to
be revealed in the last days.
*T*here is cause for rejoicing here.
You may for a time have to suffer the
distress of many trials; but this is so that
your faith, which is more precious than the
passing splendor of fire-tried gold, may by
its genuineness lead to praise, glory, and
honor when Jesus Christ appears.

1 Peter 1:3–7
Thank you for praying for me,
Love,
Samuel

Every morning Samuel would ask to go see over Blessed Mother (in my daughter's yard). He would whisper in her ear, and then he would kiss her. We believe she was with him also, and he knew who she was.

My Background Role in the Story of Samuel

In 1975 I became deeply involved in a charismatic prayer meeting at St Augustine Church in Providence, RI.

One Monday evening Beverly came and was deeply touched by the praise, prayers etc.

She and her husband, David, took the six-week life in the spirit seminar and continued to come weekly.

Indeed in 1978 they sold their home in Pawtucket and moved to Providence within a few blocks of St Augustine Church

A Community was formed called "The People of God's love". It focused on family life, family prayer etc. I enrolled their home in Pawtucket to The Sacred Heart of Jesus on October 31, 1978, and again when they moved to their new home in Providence, RI.

Beverly continues this devotion as part of her prayer life today.

I need to relate here that her husband and she were involved in other religious activities. Our conversation often turned to their deep involvement in prison ministry,

Dave and Bev have a heart for all prisoners and their families. Also, Dave and Bev were part of "The Haiti Outreach program" traveling often to Haiti to evaluate their needs and proper use of the funds that were raised for them to get clean water and to get some off the streets begging. They even broke ground for a school in Marigot that is to this day flourishing. They have a special connection with the Salesian Fathers in Haiti that do a tremendous job training young men how to build beautiful furniture.

My Role in Samuel's Birth Crisis

I was well aware that Marie, daughter of Dave and Bev, was in her first pregnancy. However, when Samuel was born, I was in Rome for the canonization of St Faustina.

As soon as I returned home and learned of the situation, I called Bev and we agreed to meet at the hospital. The nurses opened the incubator briefly, and I anointed and prayed over this little baby. While we were still there, the doctor in charge came in and told Marie and Bev that Samuel was in such a dangerous condition that they had to leave to go to Boston immediately. An ECMO machine had just become available at Massachusetts General Hospital.

Thus began four months of turmoil for them. My role was merely personal and spiritual support. I went often during the first month or so. The ECMO was a series of machines and wires. I also marveled at the small room which the hospital gave Tom and Marie to live in. There was only room for 2 reclining chairs but the hospital allowed Dave and Bev to stay with them during the four months if they could get 2 cots crammed into this tiny space.

I remember that when it was believed Samuel was dying, I travelled up to Boston with two good friends and confirmed him with the name Joseph that his parents had picked out for him.

Finally, I remember the liver transplant that saved Samuels' life. Bev does a good job of relating the details but to this day the accidental death of the young woman in CT and the transport of her liver to Boston remains a vivid memory to me.

Sincerely,
Rev. John D. Dreher

Samuel and his Dad

Samuel and Great Nana

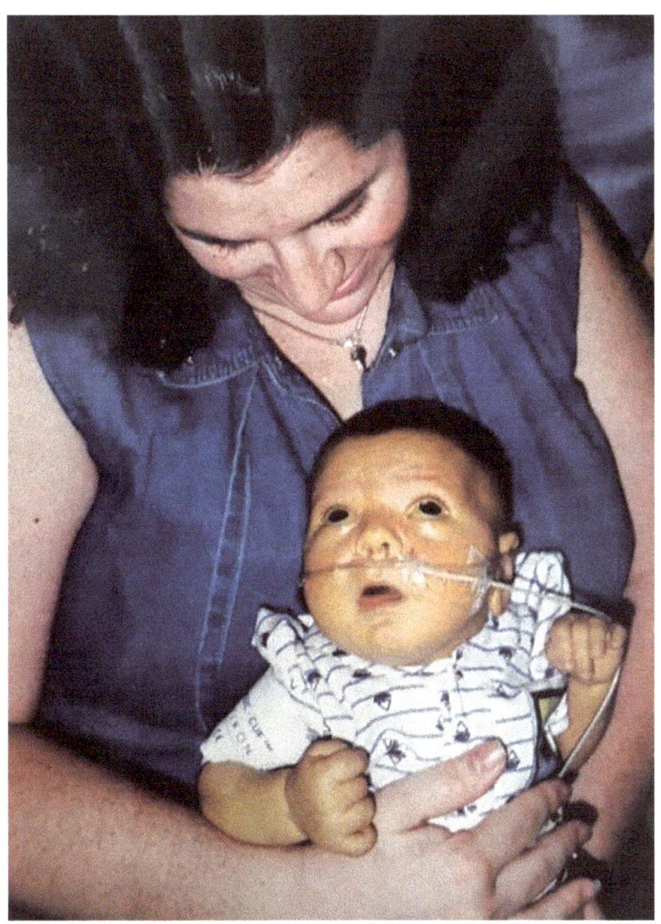

5/27/00 Marie holding Samuel first time prior to 1st transplant. You can see how jaundice/orange he was

After a brief rain shower this beautiful rainbow appeared over our home

ABOUT THE AUTHOR

Beverly Anne Munyon lives with her husband of fifty-three years in North Smithfield, Rhode Island. They have three children and nine grandchildren (two with special needs). Beverly and her husband have traveled extensively. They have made many trips to Haiti, and they broke ground for a new school in Marigot. They have also been involved in prison ministry for over fifteen years and are still involved in a limited capacity. Beverly and her husband recently bought a Havanese puppy. His name is Elyas, which is a Syrian boy's name that means "the Lord is my God." Beverly is half Syrian (therefore the naming of their puppy).